Simply Painting ™

AROUND THE WORLD

by Frank Clarke

To Jimmy, my right hand, who makes sure I am never idle. To all my friends on both sides of the Atlantic and last, but most importantly, to my family for all the support they have given in allowing me to follow my dream.

Dedication

I dedicate this book to my son Jason.

Contents

Reactions to Frank's System

Just a small sample of the mail I receive that makes it all worthwhile.

Hi Frank,
"Thought I should join your growing number of admirers from around the world, in thanking you for your wonderful program. How could anyone resist such a charming Irishman's offer to "Have some more fun"? I am having fun and find painting very relaxing. I enjoy going through your website and also seeing the artwork that would never have been painted if not for your encouragement to "try it out".
Angie Helleren, Australia

Dear Frank,
"You are a star! I took up a course of 'beginners' watercolour classes and was going to give up in disgust at my inability to paint a 3 dimensional apple! After following the instructions in your book I succeeded in producing a perfect apple - in about 10 minutes! - I am giving up the classes and spending the money on more of your books!! Thanks for my new hobby."
Kevin

Hello Frank,
"I am so excited. At 46 years old I have just discovered that you do not have to be born an artist to be able to paint really nice, frameable pictures. Thanks very much Frank for the inspiration that you give. You have an extraordinary talent!!!"
Steve Briscoe

Frank,
"I cannot thank Frank and the Simply Painting team enough. Not only have I improved my painting skills, but now feel confident enough to help and encourage others. Thank you."
Lee Terry

Dear Reader

When I took my first steps into this wonderful world of painting I realised there is an ingrained belief that painting is a gift or talent that only very few of us possess. This is, of course, absolute rubbish.

The fact is that anyone can paint a picture. All you need is the desire to do so and the more you paint the better painter you become.

With this in mind, I have taken the liberty of starting at the very beginning.

I will make you one promise. If you follow the chapters in this book, which I call the missing first five chapters,you will be able to paint by the time you finish.

Remember "anyone can paint".

So, without further ado let's **"Have Some More Fun"**!

Frank Clarke

About Frank

Frank Clarke was born in Dublin and only became a painter after retiring from business. He is now one of Ireland's most successful authors and T.V. presenters and has travelled the world teaching his Have Some More Fun method of painting.

Frank divides his time between Connemara and Dublin where he lives with his wife, Peggy, and their three sons.

Painting is not a Gift, it's a Desire

Frank did not take up the brush until he retired from a business career that included dress design, golf course management and property management.

He thought that it would be nice having a little hobby and inspired by a photograph of Winston Churchill with a glass in one hand and a paintbrush in the other, he decided to try his hand at painting.

Like many people, Frank hadn't painted anything since childhood and wondered how he would take to it many years later. At first he tried painting classes where he was immediately left behind having been told he "hadn't got the gift". Undeterred, in fact more determined that ever, he then proceeded to buy, beg and borrow all the art instruction books he could get his hands on.

Still progress was slow – something was missing. Somehow all these teachers and instructors had managed to make the same mistake. Frank recalls, "they all assumed the student, that is me, had already gained a certain level of ability. I hadn't, so where was I to start?"

"Where were the first five chapters?"

Frank's first painting!!

Well, Frank decided to start by going back to the beginning and starting with a blank sheet to teach himself the missing chapters. It was difficult at first but all was revealed when he realised that each painting could be divided into four distinct areas.

These were: the horizon, the sky, the middleground and the fore-ground. By this logical approach to building a landscape it all fell into place and suddenly Frank was painting and selling some of his landscapes of the west of Ireland. He would have happily contin-ued on this road if it wasn't for the intervention of his good friend, Harry Ellis, of the Irish Wheelchair Association.

Harry needed someone to teach his members to paint and he cajoled Frank – practically a beginner himself – to take on the job. Frank took to this task with enthusiasm and his weekly classes became "must attends" for many wheelchair members. His four-part technique was a big hit, but he did feel it was still quite difficult for beginners to remember all the basic essentials. So in a moment of inspiration *(or maybe exasperation)* he came up with the slogan

"Have Some More Fun," which means **H**orizon, **S**ky, **M**iddleground and **F**oreground. Thus the Simply Painting technique was born and Frank has never looked back.

Soon he started teaching his own classes outside the Wheelchair Association membership. These too proved immensely popular as word spread that someone had unlocked the secret that meant anyone could paint. No mystique, no gift - just a desire was all one needed.

Demand for his classes grew to such an extent that he was turning people away. It was then that Warner Home Video – a division of the Warner Bros. Studios – commissioned three videos from Frank incorporating his teaching method. Simultaneously he started working on his first book.

Both the videos and the book were to become instant success stories with his book outselling all other art books combined in its first year of publication in Ireland.

An executive of Warner Home Video also passed file tapes to RTE *(Ireland's National Broadcaster)* and they were impressed enough to commission a six-part series. Now what had started as a hobby was turning into a full time occupation. RTE commissioned more series – more books were published, more videos released. Frank has since sold over 300,000 books.

Winsor & Newton, the internationally famous art manufacturer, even created Frank's own brand of brushes exclusively designed by him to make painting with his Have Some More Fun system easier.

In 1993 the T.V. series went international airing on Discovery Channel in UK and the Learning Channel in Australia and Frank was approached by WMHT *(a PBS affiliate)* to create a further series of programmes for the US market. He has since produced one 26 part series per year and these series have screened on over 200 stations within the PBS system, Discovery in the UK, Australia, Japan, the Middle East and, of course, in Ireland where he is a household name.

As his international fame grew, so developed a loyal band of supporters who attended all his classes, bought his books and videos and the ever-growing range of Simply Painting products.

The BBC in London commissioned two 20-part series from Frank for the Arts and Crafts Hour and with that he launched his fifth book – Frank Clarke Paintbox, which reached the UK top 5 and has sold over 100,000 copies in the UK alone. Paintbox 2 was to follow quickly as the BBC was surprised by the success of the first book. They shouldn't have been, as everything that Frank touches is a success. His one-day seminars, week long courses, T.V. series, videos and books and Simply Painting website have all been unqualified successes. Over the years he has developed his unique system, always expanding its scope and complexity without leaving the beginner behind.

In this, his seventh book, he takes inspiration from the many places he has travelled while filming his Simply Painting Around the World Series. This, too, is destined to be a success, for as Frank says about his teaching method "show me someone with the desire and I will teach them to paint. I've never had a failure".

F.A. Clarke

Let's Have Some More Fun

FOUR EASY STEPS TO WONDERFUL WATERCOLOURS

Well as I always say, someone has to show you how to start and it has to be simple. When I started to teach I found the one thing all beginners, and even some amateur painters, had in common was a very disordered approach to their work.

The very same applied to me when I started to paint. I was unsure where to start and when I did, I was jumping about the paper like a bucket of frogs.

So I was determined to devise a system which students found easy to use and remember. The answer was to break down every picture into four distinct parts.

Once they did this their painting improved in leaps and bounds. However, as students left the class and did not paint again for some weeks or months, they seemed to forget what they were shown.

So I racked my brains and found what I wanted to say in a simple unforgettable sentence: -

"Have Some More Fun".

The four words represents each of the distinct parts of a painting, .ie

Have	=	Horizon
Some	=	Sky
More	=	Middleground
Fun	=	Foreground

In the following pictures you can see how the method works.

Have – Horizon
First we draw our horizon line, always straight across the paper.

Some – Sky
Then starting at the top of your picture and keeping above the horizon line, paint in the sky.

More – Middleground
Next, just above the horizon line paint in a letter "M" to represent the mountains.

Fun – Foreground
Last we paint rushes in the foreground.

Materials and Equipment

WATERCOLOUR PAINT

Watercolour paint comes in two forms – tubes and pans. I prefer to use tubes because they are moist and ready to use when squeezed onto your palette. Also tubes are easier to use with big brushes.

Pans are small squares of hard watercolour, which must be softened before use.

I use eight basic colours – *LEMON YELLOW, COBALT BLUE, ULTRAMARINE BLUE, ALIZARIN CRIMSON, LIGHT RED, RAW SIENNA, BURNT UMBER, PAYNES GREY* and a tube of white gouache.

With this selection you can mix all the other colours you will need.

These are made by Winsor & Newton and are from their Cotman range.

Before you ask where is the green paint, let me explain. Blue and yellow make green. In fact, **PAYNES GREY** and **LEMON YELLOW** make a dark green. I really believe it is better to mix your own greens.

BRUSHES

To get started you will need three brushes –

1   1.5" (38 mm) "Simply Painting Goathair Brush"
2.   0.75" (19 mm) "Simply Painting Goathair Brush"
3.   Rigger "Simply Painting Nylon Brush"

Throughout the book, I will refer to the 1.5" (38mm) as the large goathair brush and the 0.75" (19mm) as the small goathair brush.

If you can't obtain my brushes to get started use any large water-colour brush and small nylon brush you can find. You won't get the same effect, but at least you are beginning to paint.

PAPER

Watercolour paper is made in three main surfaces –

1. Rough – as the name suggests it has a rough surface.
2. Cold pressed – sometimes called Not or medium.
3. Hot pressed – which has a very smooth surface.

| 1. Rough | 2. Cold Pressed | 3. Hot Pressed |

I use Cold pressed and suggest you do the same.

Watercolour paper also comes in different thicknesses. The thickness is described in lbs.

Weight (thickness) starts at about 90 lbs (190 g) up to about 400 lbs (900 g) and the thicker the paper the higher the price.

Paper can be purchased in sheets or pads.

I recommend you use 140 lbs (300 g) in pads measuring 14" x 10" (35 cm x 25 cm) medium surface (cold pressed).

OTHER MATERIALS YOU WILL NEED

How to Control Water on the Goathair Brushes

The goathair, or obedient brush as I sometimes call it, has the ability to hold very large quantities of water. This is necessary particularly when painting large areas such as skies.

To obtain this effect when painting, simply dip the brush into the water and then into the pigment, making sure you mix up sufficient pigment to cover the area you are going to paint.

The reason for this is that if you have to stop and re-mix paint you will allow the paper to dry and you **do not** want this to happen.

When you wish to paint areas such as the middle ground of the picture, where you will require more vibrant colour – in other words more pigment, you use a cloth to remove some of the water from the body of the brush leaving the tip wet.

This is done by resting the brush flat on the cloth but leaving approximately 0.5" (1 cm) to a 1" (2.5 cm) of the brush protruding over the side so the tip remains wet.

Do this on one side of the brush and then turn the brush over and do the same on the other side. At all times ensure that the tip of the brush does not come in contact with the cloth.

For painting areas where a high amount of pigment is required and, in particular where you want the hairs of the brush to split to create rush or grass effects, it is necessary to repeat the procedure you followed for the last section, but this time include the tip of the brush when you place it on the cloth.

Controlling the water

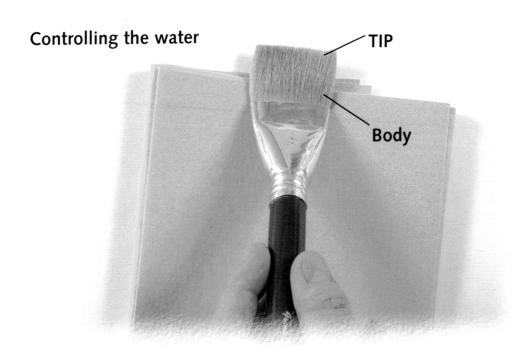

TIP

Body

The goathair brush, to my mind, is a combination of three brushes.

Firstly, you have the flat brush, which creates very large washes and can cover very big areas quickly.

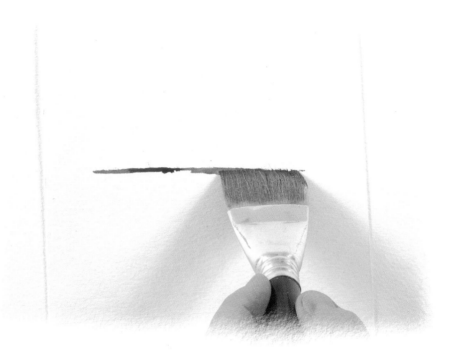

Secondly you have the point of the brush which can be used like a chisel and create middle ground effects.

Finally you have the corners, left or right, which are effective for painting trees and bushes. So it really is a three in one brush.

You also have the added advantage, unlike bristle or nylon, that my brush does not return to its original shape until made to do so and therefore you can create stippling effects.

This is where the point or top of the brush is used, loaded with pigment, and stippled onto the paper. This is particularly useful when creating foliage for trees, etc.

The small goathair brush, or "baby" goathair brush as it's sometimes called, works in exactly the same way as the larger one but on a smaller scale.

The rigger brush is a long-haired nylon brush and is very useful for detail. In fact, it is *only* useful for detail.

Very often beginners try to use the smallest brush they can because they feel more confident with it.

They think they can do less damage. This, of course, is not the case. In fact it is impossible to paint pictures of any size with a small round nylon brush, In many cases beginners' paint boxes provide only very small brushes.

These, of course, inhibit the person from producing a picture. It is also fair to explain that a nylon brush or sable will return to its original shape after each brush stroke.

You should limit the number of brushes you use. Too many brushes can only confuse and, as you have the help of the goathair brushes, it is not necessary to carry around dozens of brushes with you.

As you get more competent you can expand the range of brushes you use but always remember that the large goathair brush is the most important "friend" you have when using my system.

PEOPLE

When I started to paint I went to art exhibitions, mainly amateur ones and one of the things that struck me was the lack of figures in the paintings – even in street scenes. When I made discreet enquiries I was told that most amateur painters are afraid to include figures in their paintings because of "the fear of figure". This is a belief that figures are difficult to paint and this was why I found myself looking at street scenes with no people.

So off I went home to find a way to simplify figure painting.

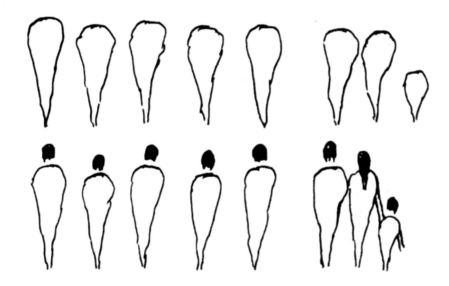

With this in mind the idea of carrots first came to me. To begin – think carrots not people. Now using the rigger brush and burnt umber paint 10 carrots.

When you have completed this exercise, starting at number one, put dots on top of the carrots. Don't make the heads too big or they will look like petrol pumps. Now you have made figures. To create female figures, draw the hair down the back.

Keep doing this exercise for 30 minutes and your carrots will improve as people. Armed with this knowledge, you can now paint figures and create scale in your painting.

TIP – Make a visit to your local art gallery and have a look at the old master pictures up close. You will find that most figures in landscape are nothing more than a blob of paint. So keep the carrots simple, that is the motto.

TIP

1 Box is for the head →

3 Box's are from the Shoulder to the waist

4 Boxs one from the waist to the feet

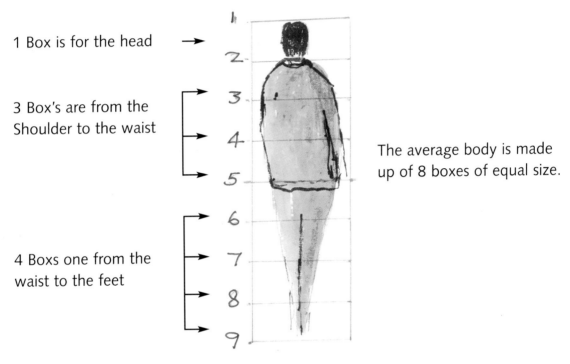

The average body is made up of 8 boxes of equal size.

This scale will help you ensure that your figures are proportionate.

MOUNTAINS

Mountains, or letter "Ms" as I call them, come in many different shapes, from rolling hills to craggy peaks. But they all have one thing in common – they are wider at the bottom than the top and they actually look like a series of letter "Ms".

Having drawn your favourite letter "M" or mountains, you can create depth by keeping the distant mountains lighter.

All you have to do is paint in your mountain range and let it dry.

Then using the same colour go over the mountain you want to appear closer.

You can repeat this exercise as many times as you want.

MISTY MOUNTAINS

Every landscape painter loves to paint misty mountains.

First, paint your sky. While it is still wet, using a clear
Painting goathair brush, take out some pigr
dry.

Now paint your maintains (letter "Ms"). Then using the large
Simply Painting goathair brush repeat the action you used to make
the clouds.

Lesson One

A LAKE IN THE WEST OF IRELAND

Our first picture is what I call my basic landscape. It shows how the Simply Painting "Have Some More Fun" system works.

In this picture we keep colour mixing to the minimum. When you have completed painting this picture you will have learned the basics of landscape painting and my advice to you is to repeat this picture a couple of times. It will get you used to painting skies, mountains, middlegrounds, water and foregrounds.

TIP – why not give all your friends a landscape. While making them happy you will be gaining valuable practice.

Materials – paints: *COBALT BLUE, LEMON YELLOW, BURNT UMBER.*

Brushes: 1.5" (38 mm) Large Simply Painting brush, Simply Painting rigger brush.

Paper: a sheet of 14" x 10" (35 cm x 25 cm) watercolour paper 140 lb (300 g).

A water container (a large one is best), a palette to put your paint on (a large white plate will do), some cloths, a pencil, an eraser, a ruler and masking tape. You will need a stiff board to affix your paper to.

It needs to be approximately 12" x 16" (30 cm x 39 cm). And a hairdryer if you have one.

Start by affixing your paper to the board then raise the board approximately 2" (5 cm) at the back by placing something under it.

HORIZON – now take your pencil and ruler and draw the horizon line about 3" (7 cm) up from the bottom of the paper.

Put some ***COBALT BLUE*** paint out on your palette. Then dip the large goathair brush into the water and mix some blue paint.

SKY – now starting from the top of the paper using broad strokes paint down to within 1" (2 cm) of the horizon line.

Now stop, don't fiddle. Let the sky dry. Use your hairdryer if you like.

TIP – remember you have two minutes to paint the sky, so don't be tempted to over paint it.

Mountains, or my letter "M's" are next. Always paint them a little wobbly.

Using your large goathair brush mix a little **BURNT UMBER**, with mostly **COBALT BLUE**.

TIP – look at my picture to compare your colour mix.

Now paint the mountains. Do it with the least possible strokes, making sure you leave approximately 1" (2.5 cm) between the bottom of the mountains and the horizon line. Once again let the mountains dry.

MIDDLEGROUND – now for the middleground. First clean the brush, then dry the body of the brush.

Now mix some *LEMON YELLOW* with a little *BURNT UMBER* and paint across the space between the mountain and the horizon line. You can go a little up the mountains but make sure you don't go below the horizon.

Next add some *BURNT UMBER* to create darker areas particularly along the riverbank. Dry the middleground.

FOREGROUND – the water is next so first clean your brush.

With the same mixture used to paint the mountains, *COBALT BLUE* with a little *BURNT UMBER*, with broad strokes paint the water.

TIP

TIP – when painting the water make sure you go all the way across the paper without stopping.

The reeds come next. First clean and dry your large goathair brush. Then dip into the **LEMON YELLOW** and using downward strokes paint across the bottom of your picture.

Now without cleaning your brush add some **BURNT UMBER** and repeat.

At this stage there are only a couple of things to do to complete your first picture. First the bird. I call him my friend Joe.

With the rigger brush make an inky mixture of **BURNT UMBER** and paint a flat letter "V". That's all there is to it.

Now sign your picture, mount and frame it. Well done. You have completed your first watercolour landscape!

ANIMALS AND BIRDS

It is almost considered an advanced painting course when we mention animals. But this is not the case, providing we simplify them as we did with the human form.

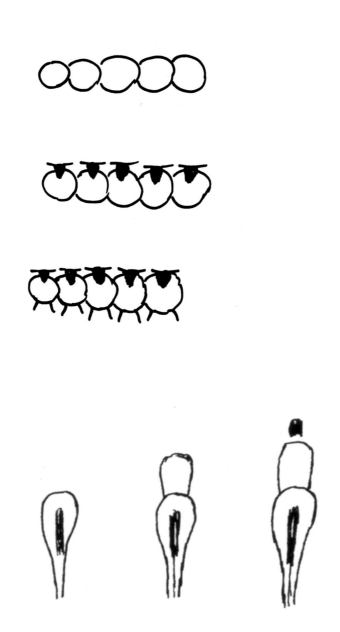

With a little bit of practice you can create a parrot from a carrot!

Start with the letter "R" and add a head and tail.

A swan is like the number "2".

TREES

Trees are essential parts of landscape painting and, of course, there are many different types and shapes of trees. So let's get started.

First go out and look at – and then paint – a tree. Always look at the subject you are going to paint for at least 5 minutes before you start to paint it.

Compare how tall the tree is to how wide it is, how big the trunk is and the overall shape and colouring, before you make any effort to paint it. This exercise is to give your brain time to take it all in.

TREE EXERCISE

Pine trees are painted using the corner of the goathair brush.

A tree can be many colours. This one is painted with **ALIZARIN CRIMSON** and **LEMON YELLOW** for the leaves using the stippling method. This is a downward dabbing of the large goathair brush. The brush must be almost dry.

Old tree trunks. Paint your sky, let it dry and then wet the area where you want the old tree to be. Now while it is still wet paint the stump and you will get a fuzzy edge on your tree.

To reproduce the different colours in this hedgerow – use the small goathair brush. This is an exercise in colour mixing!

Lesson Two

WOODLAND SCENE IN PINK

Materials required –

Paint: *ALIZARIN CRIMSON, LIGHT RED, LEMON YELLOW, BURNT UMBER, RAW SIENNA.*

Brushes: Large Simply Painting goathair brush, small Simply Painting goathair brush, Simply Painting rigger.

Paper: 1 sheet 14" x 10" (35 cm x 25 cm), 140 lb (300 g) water-colour paper.

Palette or white plate, a water container, a pencil, a ruler, masking tape, some tissue paper, some cloths and a stiff board 12" x 16" (30 cm x 39 cm)

Affix your paper to the board longways – we are painting land-scape.

Horizon – using your ruler and pencil draw the horizon line approximately 3" (7 cm) up the paper.

Now using the large goathair brush, make up a mixture of *ALIZARIN CRIMSON* and *LIGHT RED*, about half of each and starting from the top of the paper paint down to the horizon line.

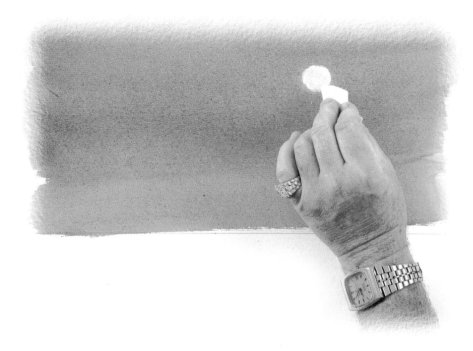

Now while the paper is still wet, using a piece of folded tissue
paper, dab out the moon.

TIP – make sure you have the tissue paper ready
before you start to paint the sky.

Middleground – when the sky is dry, using a mixture of **ALIZARIN CRIMSON** and **LIGHT RED**, paint the mountains, making sure you keep above the horizon line.

Let the mountains dry and with a mixture of **RAW SIENNA** and **BURNT UMBER**, about half of each, using the small goathair brush, paint in the middleground. Now let it dry.

Take the large goathair brush and clean it. Then using **_LEMON YEL-LOW_** (make a light mixture) paint the field under the mountains. Let the field dry.

TIP – If you have one, use a hairdryer to dry your painting.

Foreground – now let's start on the foreground. Using the corner of the small goathair brush, with a mixture of *RAW SIENNA* and *BURNT UMBER*, dab in the hedge. Then add in some *BURNT UMBER* to darken and create shadows.

With the same mixture, using the large goathair brush paint in the bushes on the left side of the picture.

Create some branches in the bushes. This is done by using your fingernail to scrape in an upward direction.

Now, it's time to paint the large trees on the right side of the picture. Do this with the small goathair brush, and a mixture of **BURNT UMBER** and **RAW SIENNA**. Paint the tree trunks.

Then change to the rigger brush to paint some smaller branches. Add a little **BURNT UMBER** to the right of the trees to create shadows.

Now comes the part of the picture I really enjoy – the foliage. This is where the goathair brush really comes into its own. First dry your brush, and then dip it into the **LIGHT RED** paint and then using downward strokes with the tip of the brush stipple the leaves. Now add some **BURNT UMBER.**

Paint the foreground under the trees using a mixture of **RAW SIEN-NA** and **BURNT UMBER**. Using broad strokes with the large goathair brush go right across the paper. Add in some **BURNT UMBER** to create tufts of grass.

Now the fence. Paint it with the rigger brush, using **BURNT UMBER**. Don't make the fence posts too straight. Join them with the rigger using **BURNT UMBER**.

Put a small bush in the middle using the rigger. Finish by adding the bird, if you like, and sign your picture.

WATER

There are many different types of water action.

(1) Still Water

To get this effect simply draw the brush across the paper in one single stroke. Remember water reflects the colour of the sky.

(2) Fast Flowing Water

Fast flowing water always runs downhill and is best painted coming towards you. Leaving some of the white paper showing creates the effect of broken or white water.

F.A.Clarke

Flowing water can also be created by adding white gouache when the paper is dry.

Add a line at back

Join the front to the back

Join right front top to bottom

Sailboats

Sailboats add a certain something to your seascapes. Paint them with white gouache using the rigger.

BRIDGES

A basic bridge is very simple.

It is a letter "U" upside down, with a curved line over it to represent the walkway.

Thicken and darken one side of the "U" to create the impression of depth and shadow.

Add in trees and fencing to give your painting perspective.

BUILDINGS

A cottage, a log cabin, a barn, a two-storey house all have the same basic shape. In fact, almost all buildings have a roof, wall, window and door.

So we start off by painting two inverted "Vs" and then joining them.

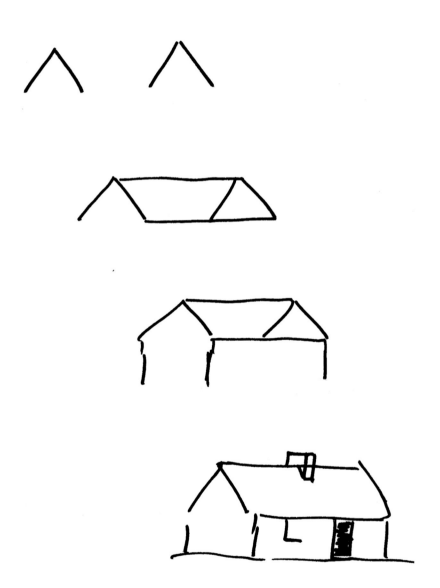

Shade in the roof, doors and windows.

Cottage walls are usually white but you can colour the walls in any colour to create a barn or cabin.

TIP

Always place your point of interest – the cottage in this case – off-centre.

LIGHT AND SHADOW

Light and shade bring your painting to life. Don't worry about knowing how to use this skill, as it will come with practice. The fact is that when you start to paint you begin to see with an artist's eye.

Without light and shadow

With light and shadow

Lesson Three

RIVER IN WALES

This painting is from a television programme I shot in Wales and it's one I won't forget. The river runs through the grounds of a famous house owned by the Ladies of Llangollen. Many famous people stayed there including the Duke of Wellington on his way to the Battle of Waterloo. It was also nearly the Waterloo of our camera-man Mike who fell into the river. However, being a true professional, he held the camera over his head, therefore saving our television shoot!

Materials - paint: *ULTRAMARINE BLUE, LEMON YELLOW, , BURNT UMBER, LIGHT RED, PAYNE'S GREY* and *WHITE GOUACHE.*

Brushes: Large Simply Painting goathair brush, small Simply Painting goathair brush and Simply Painting rigger brush.

Paper: a sheet of 14" x 10" (35 cm x 25 cm) watercolour paper, 140 lb (300 g).

Water container (a large one is best), a palette to put your paint on (a large white plate will do), some cloths, a pencil, an eraser, a ruler, masking tape, a stiff board to affix your paper to (it needs to be approximately 12" x 16" (30 cm x 39 cm) and a hairdryer, if you have one.

This picture is painted in portrait. So we start by taking a sheet of watercolour paper and affixing it to our board upright.

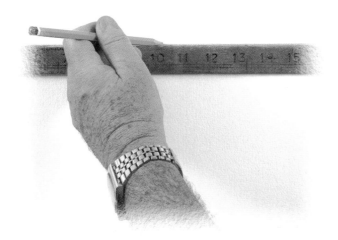

Using the ruler and pencil draw the horizon line 5.5" (13.5 cm) up the paper. Then make sure you raise the board by placing something under the back of it.

TIP – this picture, like all watercolours, is painted light to dark. This means using light colours first and adding darker ones.

Start at the top of the paper and paint a light mixture of **ULTRAMARINE BLUE**, using the larger goathair brush. Then add some **LEMON YELLOW** while the paper is still wet. Now add some **RAW SIENNA**. There is no need to clean your brush just make sure it's not too wet.

Stop approximately 1" (2.5 cm) above the horizon line. Start again at the top of the paper and add in some extra **ULTRAMARINE BLUE** to the **LEMON YELLOW** leaving the centre alone. Repeat on the right side. Now go down each side.

Start to darken the left side.

Now start building up colour on the right side of the picture

Don't go below the horizon.

Start to add darker colour without cleaning your brush.

Now just above the
horizon line, where
you left the gap,
using **RAW SIENNA**
only, go right across
the paper with the
large goathair brush.

You can now scrape some
branches with your nail on
each side.

To finish the top half of your painting take the rigger brush and using **BURNT UMBER** paint in some branches.

It is now time to paint your water using **COBALT BLUE** and **RAW SIENNA**. With the small goathair brush, make broad strokes about 2" (5 cm) down the paper.

Now start to drag the brush down to give the impression of water cascading down.

Now when the water is dry, go over the top part again, adding in some darker colour to the cascade.

Let's start to paint
some rocks in the river
with a mixture of
PAYNE'S GREY and
BURNT UMBER.

Have a good look at
the finished picture
(P.71) to see where
the rocks are placed.

Darken the left side of the rocks using **PAYNE'S GREY.**

With your rigger brush and some **WHITE GOUACHE.** add in some white water around the rocks.

And on the cascade too.

Darken the water by adding some **COBALT BLUE** with a little **PAYNE'S GREY**.

Now it's time for Joe the bird, and to sign your picture.

FIXING - After you have signed your painting don't touch it. Any "fixing" can ruin it.

You can test your painting by placing a matt over it as I do. You will be amazed how much better it makes it. My motto is never let anyone see your picture until it's framed. So go on and get yours framed!

Lesson Four

OLD COTTAGE BY THE LAKE

There are very few of these old cottages left in Ireland. I suppose it's called progress. But travelling around the western coastline of Ireland you can still stumble across these enchanting structures in splendid isolation. This one is near Clifden in the west of Ireland.

Materials – paint: *RAW SIENNA, LEMON YELLOW, LIGHT RED, COBALT BLUE, BURNT UMBER.*

Brushes: Large Simply Painting goathair brush, small Simply Painting goathair brush, Simply Painting rigger brush.

Paper: sheet of 14" x 10" (35 cm x 25 cm) watercolour paper, 140 lbs (300 g).

Masking fluid and old brush. A water container (a large one is best), a palette to put your paint on (a large white plate will do), some cloths, a pencil, an eraser, a ruler, masking tape, and a stiff board to affix your paper to (this needs to be approximately 12" x 16" (30 cm x 39 cm). And a hairdryer, if you have one.

Take your sheet of 14" x 10" paper and affix it to the board long-ways (landscape). Make sure you raise the back of the board about 2".

Horizon – now draw the horizon line about 3.5" (9 cm) up from the bottom of the paper. Don't put the pencil away as you will need it to draw the cottage.

Masking fluid is used to protect part of your painting while you paint in backgrounds. It is a liquid rubber compound and comes in a bottle. Let's say you want to protect a cottage while painting the mountains in the background. It's easy, just cover the cottage with masking fluid, then let it dry and when you have completed the mountain simply rub off the masking fluid and you have a perfect outline of the cottage.

Now paint over the cottage with masking fluid and let the masking fluid dry.

TIP - To avoid damaging your brush when using masking fluid, it is important to clean it every 20 seconds, otherwise it will become clotted and damaged

Sky – we can now start to paint the sky. To begin put the **RAW SIENNA**, **COBALT BLUE** and **LIGHT RED** out on your palette. With the large goathair make up a feint mix of **RAW SIENNA** and paint down to the horizon,

Lastly mix some **COBALT BLUE** and some **LIGHT RED**, mostly **COBALT BLUE**, and paint top of sky. Now let the sky dry.

Paint it using a mixture of **COBALT BLUE** and **BURNT UMBER** with the rigger brush. Don't forget the rope.

To finish use some **WHITE GOUACHE** to paint bog cotton, the white flowers.

Last, but by no means least, Joe, the bird.

Now sign and frame your picture.

Lesson Five

WAY OUT WEST

You know I feel very lucky getting to travel around the world while shooting my TV series. I have had the opportunity to visit many wonderful locations. This lonely rock formation is from a pro-gramme I made in Arizona in the mid west of America.

The materials needed are:

Paint: *RAW SIENNA, LEMON YELLOW, ULTRAMARINE BLUE, BURNT UMBER, PAYNE'S GREY*.

Masking fluid

1 sheet 14" x 10 " (35 cm x 25 cm) watercolour paper, 140 lb (300 g)

A palette, a pencil, a ruler, masking tape, a water container and some cloths.

A board to affix your paper on approx. 12" x 14" (30 cm x 35 cm).

So let's Have Some More Fun –

Horizon line – with a pencil and ruler draw the horizon line 4" (10 cm) up the paper.

Middleground – Now rub off the masking fluid, always working towards the centre of the rocks in case the paper tears.

Next, with the rigger brush, using *RAW SIENNA*, paint the right hand side of the rocks. With a mixture of *BURNT UMBER* and *LIGHT RED* paint the dark side of the rocks.

Change to the small goathair brush. With a mixture of *RAW SIEN-NA* and a little *LEMON YELLOW* start to paint down below the horizon line.

TIP

TIP – for best effects the brush needs to be almost dry.

The bush on the left is next. Dry your large goathair brush and mix up some *RAW SIENNA* and *LIGHT RED.* Then, starting at the bottom, dab the paint on your picture using the corner of the brush. Add some darker colour to the bottom of the bush.

While the paper is still wet scrape out some branches using your *nailbrush* (your finger!).

Let's now start in the middle of the picture and paint the bushes, which are in the light, using a mixture of *LEMON YELLOW* and *COBALT BLUE*. Use the large goathair brush to paint the bushes.

Now with a mixture of *LEMON YELLOW* and *COBALT BLUE* and the large goathair brush, go across the bottom of the picture using broad strokes.

To finish the foreground use the large goathair brush and make some downward strokes using **_BURNT UMBER_**. The brush needs to be quite dry for this.

Now it's time for Joe, the bird, or your flat letter "V".

Well done. Another masterpiece.

FLOWERS

There is a divide among artists. Some paint landscapes, others paint flowers.

It is probably fair to say ladies are more likely to paint flowers than men.

However, there is no doubt that watercolour as a medium is ideal for painting flowers as they look as good as the main subject matter themselves or as part of a larger landscape.

Start with the simplest form of flower.

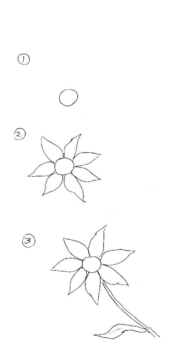

TIP - Get a gardening book or buy a bunch of flowers. Always remember it is easier to paint something you can see.

Lesson Six

LILAC LESSON

While walking through an artstore the other day, I picked up a sheet of black paper and wondered what a watercolour would look like painted on it. So, having purchased some, I went home and started to play around with it. Then the idea came to me: how about using watercolour mixed with white gouache? Gouache makes watercolour opaque (you can see it on a dark surface) and it was then I realised how easy it was to paint on coloured paper. Not only that but it was a very easy way of creating lovely pictures – and what fun! For this lesson I have used black paper, but you could use a different colour paper – even white.

Materials you need

1   One sheet black paper – A4 11" x 8" (27.5 cm x 20 cm) or the nearest size you can obtain

2   Simply Painting rigger brush

Small Simply Painting goathair brush

3   *LEMON YELLOW, RAW SIENNA, COBALT BLUE* and *WHITE GOUACHE.*

4   A water container, palette (white plate), some old cloths, a stiff board 12" x 9" (30 cm x 23 cm) at least, masking tape and a sheet of kitchen paper.

TIP **Put the paint out on your palette, keep it to the side. This leaves you room to mix paint in the centre of your palette.**

Take a sheet of black paper and affix it to your board in portrait (upright).

Raise the back of the board about 2" by placing something under it.

With the Simply Painting rigger brush paint in the branches of the lilac bush using *RAW SIENNA* and a little *WHITE GOUACHE*.

Again with the small goathair brush paint some leaves using lots of *LEMON YELLOW* and a little *COBALT BLUE*.

Add some single leaves using the rigger brush.

HOW TO MAKE A BRUSH OUT OF A SHEET OF KITCHEN PAPER

Take a sheet of kitchen paper and fold it in half.

Now fold in half again

Next roll it like a cigar
and

Now using the jagged
end dip it into your
paint

Now take a sheet of kitchen paper towel and fold it as shown on pages 95 and 96. Dip it into the **COBALT BLUE**, add a little **WHITE GOUACHE** and dab with the paper to make lilac blooms.

Now add some lilac blooms to the left.

Now add some **WHITE GOUACHE** to the piece of kitchen towel and dab on right side of blooms to create the effect that light is coming from the right.

Next with a mixture of **RAW SIENNA** and **WHITE GOUACHE** dab in the ear of corn.

Add some twigs with a mixture of *RAW SIENNA* and *WHITE GOUACHE*. Use the rigger brush.

Now sign your master-piece. Use *WHITE GOUACHE* and the rigger brush to sign your name. Add plenty of water to make the gouache inky.

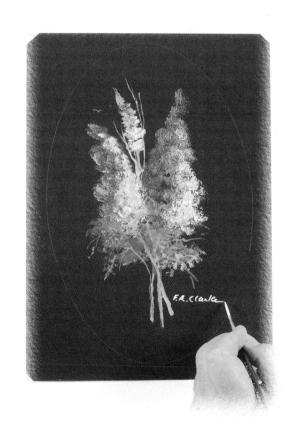

Well done.

You can obtain an oval matt in any good framing store.

Lesson Seven

SNOWY MOUNTAIN SCENE

Materials you need:

1 Sheet ordinary black paper at least 190 g A4 (11" x 8")

Paint: *WHITE GOUACHE, RAW SIENNA, LEMON YELLOW, COBALT BLUE, BURNT UMBER*

Brushes: Small Simply Painting goathair brush, Simply Painting rigger brush

Palette (white plate), a bottle top, masking tape, a stiff board of at least 12" x 9"

Take the sheet of black paper and affix it to your board in landscape (long ways).

Draw your horizon line about 3" (7.5 cm) up the paper.

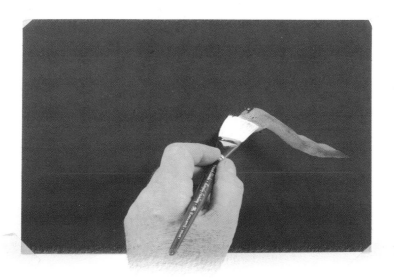

Using the small goathair brush, paint in the mountains. Use a little *WHITE GOUACHE* to give a feint effect, making sure not to go below the horizon line.

3. Next clean your brush and using strong **WHITE GOUACHE** paint the mountain tops.

4. Mix **LEMON YELLOW** and **COBALT BLUE** with very little **WHITE GOUACHE** and using the small goathair brush paint down to the horizon line to give a green hue.

5. Now using the small goathair brush with a mixture of **COBALT BLUE** and **WHITE GOUACHE** paint the lake under the mountains and let it dry.

6. Clean the brush and dry it. Then with a mixture of **RAW SIENNA** and very little **WHITE GOUACHE,** using downward strokes, paint the reeds around the lake. Next add some **BURNT UMBER** to darken the reeds.

7. Now for the moon. Make up a weak mixture of **WHITE GOUACHE** by adding some water. Then take your bottle top and dip the open side into the paint. Now lightly stamp it on the paper.

If you prefer you can use a coin by placing it on the paper and drawing around it with a pencil.

8. Now use the rigger brush to fill in the moon.

9. You can now create some reflections on the lake with **WHITE GOUACHE** using the rigger brush.

10. Now sign it with the rigger brush and some *WHITE GOUACHE*.

These small paintings on coloured paper make ideal gifts and cards for special friends and family.

TIP

To make a greeting card, first fold the paper in half, then paint the picture. You can use a matt spray to fix your work and stop it smudging.

Choosing your Frame

A frame can make a picture. Every artist knows this, so it is imperative that you frame your work. Always carry a matt (mount) with you. The inside opening needs to be 9.5" x 13.5" when using 10" x 14" (35 cm x 25 cm) paper. Also make sure you sign well in from the side of the paper otherwise the mount will cover the signature. Your local frame shop will be happy to help you.

TIP – Always frame your picture before you show it to your friends.

Make your own Colour Chart

What is a colour chart (sometimes called a colour wheel)?

It is a chart used by artists to record their colour mixes. It saves them having to test colour mixes each time they paint.

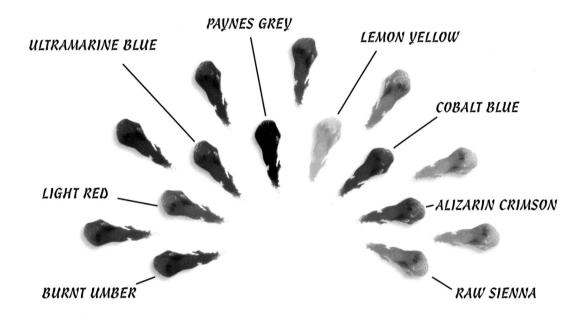

PAYNES GREY

ULTRAMARINE BLUE

LEMON YELLOW

COBALT BLUE

LIGHT RED

ALIZARIN CRIMSON

BURNT UMBER

RAW SIENNA

All you have to do to create your own colour chart is to mix each of your eight colours with one another e.g.

COBALT BLUE + LEMON YELLOW	=	green
ALIZARIN CRIMSON + COBALT BLUE	=	purple
LEMON YELLOW + ALIZARIN CRIMSON	=	orange

The reason I have left the colour chart until now is my belief that you paint first and make charts later. I can remember attending a painting class where the teacher made us make a colour chart first before we were allowed to paint and I found it BORING.

So my advice is to make your chart in your own time.

Preparing for a Field Trip

There is nothing more frustrating than arriving at your favourite painting spot to find that you have forgotten something important. To make sure this doesn't happen I have prepared a checklist. This list is hanging in my studio and before I leave I always check. Here it is.

1. Paints (bring extra tubes) and white gouache
2. Brushes
3. Paper
4. Palette
5. Cloths
6. Water container
7. Water
8. Board
9. Stool/seat
10. Masking tape
11. Ruler, pencil, eraser
12. Easel
13. View Finder
14. Waterproofs (jacket and pants)
15. Umbrella (you never know)
16. Flask of tea
17. Camera and film
18. Sandwiches/snacks
19. Walkman
20. And a bag for all your rubbish!

You might like to make your own list. I promise it will save you much heartache.

Using a Camera

Many so-called art experts will tell you it is wrong to use a camera. My advice is don't listen to them. These experts usually aren't painters themselves; otherwise they would not make such silly statements. The use of a camera can be a fantastic help when you sit down later to paint. Use your camera as a sketchbook.

When you want to paint the picture get the photograph you took and then refine it to make a better picture. It might be necessary to remove an unsightly billboard or move a mountain slightly.

Always try to use a photograph you took yourself as you are refreshing your memory of the scene. As you have actually been to the scene you are about to paint it is much easier; also it is your photograph and you are not copying someone else's. So use your camera as your sketchbook. Remember if the camera had been available in the time of Constable, Vermeer or Michelangelo, I am sure they would have used it.

The Camera

With the avent of Digital Cameras a real advance for artists you are not tied to film and the cost of same, you can go out and take as many photos as you want and go home and delete the pictures you dont require. I often go out and take dozens of pictures of skies when i return home i can view them on my computer and only keep the one's i require.

TIP – When you take your photograph make a note of the colours, as photographs sometimes don't reflect the correct colour.

Extra Pictures to Paint

Here are a selection from my television programmes – Simply Painting Around the World – for you to paint using the "Have Some More Fun" system.

All are painted on 14" x 10" (35 cm x 25 cm) paper.

BOGLANDS OF IRELAND

I captured this scene early one morning while walking along the bog in Connemara.

As the name suggests this is a painting of boglands, which are areas of swampland, created, believe it or not by man.
When the early settler came to Ireland they cut down the vast forests to build homes and ships, and to clean the land for agriculture.
Now unfortunately, the trees soaked up the rain and also protected the land from excessive wetness, when the trees were gone the rain fell directly onto the land and the iron contained in the soil, was washed down until it met the rocks creating a non porous plain, so the land flooded and created a swap, which over the years turned the soil and the roots of the trees into turf.

We now cut the turf, let it dry, and use it for fuel, so when you go around Ireland you will see cottages with turf stacked up against the end wall, to be used in the winter to heat and cook with.

These's piles of turf are called "Ricks of turf"

Colours: **ALIZARIN CRIMSON, COBALT BLUE, BURNT UMBER, RAW SIENNA** and **LEMON YELLOW**.

1. Draw the horizon line 4.5" (11 cm) up the paper.2. Paint the sky starting at the bottom with a strip of **LEMON YELLOW** next add **ALIZARIN CRIMSON**, then **COBALT BLUE**. Use the large goathair brush.

3. Mountain – **COBALT BLUE** plus a little **RAW SIENNA**.

4. Middleground – using the small goathair brush paint middleground with **BURNT UMBER** plus **COBALT BLUE**.

5. Foreground – using the large goathair brush paint a strip of **ALIZARIN CRIMSON** and underneath a strip of **LEMON YELLOW** to show reflections in stream. Let it dry. Now paint the rushes using an almost dry large goathair brush with **RAW SIENNA**. Then add some **BURNT UMBER**. Make sure you leave a gap to show the stream.

DESERT CACTUS, NEW MEXICO

Colours: *ALIZARIN CRIMSON*, *BURNT UMBER*, *LEMON YELLOW*, *RAW SIENNA* and *LIGHT RED*.

Draw the horizon line about 3.5" (9 cm) up the paper.

First sketch in the cactus with a pencil.

Sky – paint a strip of *LEMON YELLOW* across the bottom of the sky just above the horizon line. Now add *ALIZARIN CRIMSON* and *LIGHT RED* using the large goathair brush. Let the paper dry.

Paint the mountain using *ALIZARIN CRIMSON* and *BURNT UMBER*.

Paint foreground with *RAW SIENNA* and a little *LIGHT RED*.

Paint in the cactus using *LIGHT RED* and *BURNT UMBER*.

Paint the bush using *BURNT UMBER*.

ARIZONA MESA

A flat topped rock formation in the mid west.

Paint the sky using **COBALT BLUE.**

Paint the flat-topped mountain using a **BURNT UMBER** and **LIGHT RED** mixture.

The middleground is created using a mixture of **RAW SIENNA, LEMON YELLOW**, and **COBALT BLUE** for the grass.

Paint the foreground. The trees are painted with the large goathair brush using a mixture of **COBALT BLUE** and **LEMON YELLOW** and using your nail to scratch out the tree trunks. Darken the bottom of the trees using **BURNT UMBER**.

SENAGUA

Just outside Jerome.

Draw in horizon line – 3.5" (9.5 cm) up the paper

Paint the sky using a mixture of *RAW SIENNA* and *COBALT BLUE*

Paint the mountains using *COBALT BLUE* and *LIGHT RED*

Paint middleground using *RAW SIENNA*

The bush on the left is painted using *COBALT BLUE, LEMON YELLOW, RAW SIENNA* and *BURNT UMBER*

To paint in the river use *COBALT BLUE*

The foreground is painted using *RAW SIENNA* and *LEMON YELLOW*

And finally paint the trees on the right with a mixture of *RAW SIENNA, LEMON YELLOW, COBALT BLUE, LIGHT RED* and *BURNT UMBER.*

FOREST LESSON

Here is a similar picture to "Woodland Scene in Pink," only this time I have used different colours. Try it.

The colours used are

1. **ULTRAMARINE BLUE** for the sky

2. **RAW SIENNA** and **ULTRAMARINE BLUE** for the mountains

3. **RAW SIENNA** for the middleground

4. **ULTRAMARINE BLUE** and **LEMON YELLOW** for the trees and bushes, then adding some **BURNT UMBER**.

5. The ditch is painted with **RAW SIENNA** and **BURNT UMBER**

6. The fence is **BURNT UMBER**

7. The foreground is **RAW SIENNA, LEMON YELLOW** and **COBALT BLUE**. Finally, add some **BURNT UMBER.**

ROCKS ON A BEACH

These rocks were part of a painting I did for a television show I made in Co. Kerry, Ireland. So you can see that you can take a small subject or part of a larger picture to make a fresh painting.

Colours: **COBALT BLUE, RAW SIENNA, BURNT UMBER**, plus masking fluid

Rocks – First draw the rocks, then paint over with masking fluid.

When dry, paint the sky with **COBALT BLUE**.

Next paint the beach with **RAW SIENNA.**

Let them dry, then rub off the masking fluid.

Now paint the rocks with **COBALT BLUE** and **BURNT UMBER**. Start light by adding water, then add darker colour using less water.

Quick Fix

Most people believe that you can't fix mistakes in watercolours. This is simply not true.

Fault

Your sky is a mess

Fix

Wet the complete sky with the large goathair brush filled with water. You can now repair the sky. This must be done before you start the mountains. If you're still not happy, just turn your paper over and start again – you only lost two minutes.

Fault

You want to remove part of the picture while leaving the rest untouched.

Fix

Run the cold water tap on the portion of the picture you want to remove with the brush. You will notice that the pigment will run off the paper leaving the rest of the picture untouched. Let the picture dry and then continue painting.

Fault

You have made a mistake with your masking fluid and some of your painting is now covered in a colour when it should have been left white.

Fix

Get some white gouache and paint over the area.

Fault

There is a dark mark on your picture and you want to remove it.

Fix

Take the small rigger brush and wet the mark with clean water. Then gently agitate the area you want to remove. Now get a tissue and dab in the area. You may need to repeat this process several times.

Fault

You forgot to paint a cottage or want to add some sheep to the finished painting.

Fix

Let the picture dry and then repaint with white gouache.

Fault

Part of your picture is good and part poor.

Fix

Cut out the good part and frame it you may laugh but this is a trick often used by artists.

Fault

Your horizon line is not straight this particularly applies to a seascape.

Fix

Rather than trying to retouch the sea. Frame the picture making sure the horizon line is straight this will mean the picture is slightly crooked but that's ok.

Complementary: The complementary of a primary colour is the combination of the two remaining primaries, e.g. in paints, blue and yellow mixed give green, which is the complementary of red. Mixing complementaries, for example, red and green, makes deep, intense darks (blacks, browns and dark greys).

Mediums

Mediums are used to create an even wider variety of techniques and effects when mixed with watercolours.

Gum Arabic

Adding Gum Arabic to a watercolour wash will have the following effects:

Increase transparency and gloss to give greater brilliance of colour.

Reduce the staining of pigments, making washes easier to lift.

Ox Gall

A few drops of Ox Gall added to your water pot will improve the wetting and flow of your first watercolour washed onto any hard sized papers. On soft sized papers it may increase the staining power of some pigments.

Statements to Remember

1. I can do that.

2. Art is for all of us.

3. It is fair to say that the best painter never painted a picture and the best writer never wrote a book. Why? Because they never tried.

4. Einstein failed maths. At school.

5. Many people paint with their foot or their mouth because they have some disability. So if they can, why can't you?

6. Notice how long artists, writers, poets live. They have an active brain and are doing something they love to do.

7. Painting will encourage you to see for the first time trees, mountains and your surroundings. You will develop an artist's eye.

8. Be a friend. Tell a friend about the fun you are having with your new hobby.

9. Don't worry about originality. Your originality will shine through no matter what you do.

10. Think can't and you won't. Be positive.

11. Think of painting, picture colours, brushes, etc. Now at the same time try to think of something nasty but don't wipe out the nice picture. You can't, can you?

12. Learning to paint is learning to see.

My Parting Words

Dear Friend,

I am sure having read the book you are now saying to yourself "I can do that." Well, do it. I made you a promise at the start of the book and if you have followed the instructions you will have realised that painting is á desire not a gift and anyone can do it.

I hope you now realise the importance of the first five chapters that I referred to. It may seem silly to compare a painting book to a cookery book, but in some ways they are similar. Both should list the materials you need and how to use them in as simple a way as possible.

I am lucky to have the pleasure of teaching all ages to paint. I can assure you the biggest barrier to beginners is not their ability to paint but getting them to say, "I can do that." I hope by now you already believe you can.

So enjoy your new hobby. You will find it one of the most therapeutic and satisfying of pastimes. There is a saying – you will never be lonely with a paintbrush. "Believe me" it's so true!

So till we meet again, Have Some More Fun.

Frank Clarke

Till we meet again

To have some *MORE* fun,

visit my website:

and my online Painting School

@

www.simplypainting.com